THE UK AIR FRYER COOKBOOK 2023

1000 days of quick and delicious traditional English recipes for beginners and pros.
Tips and tricks for perfect frying

DAPHNE WHITE

Introduction

As Air Fryers has been introduced to the UK market, the demand for healthy, delicious and safe recipes has never been so high. THE UK AIR FRYER COOKBOOK 2023 is designed to give you an extensive collection of air fryer recipes tailored to the UK market. This will include both traditional favourites and exciting new ideas for you to try in your own home. Taking inspiration from renowned chefs, this book provides easy-to-follow instructions for a variety of dishes from breakfast through to dessert.

As air fryers have skyrocketed in popularity, more and more companies are producing their own models of all different shapes and sizes. With so many different choices, each with its own unique features, it can be intimidating to anyone new to (or even familiar with) air frying. In this cookbook, we aim to provide simple, accessible information on air frying with recipes designed to help beginners achieve their goals with little effort. We will also provide tips and techniques for getting the most out of your air fryer, including some of our own hacks and tricks. This book is designed to be used as a reference guide with the recipes and background information all easily accessible and within reach.

We hope that, with our recipes and guidance, you too can enjoy the many benefits of air frying in your own kitchen. So, whether you are a first-time air fryer or an experienced professional, we hope that this book will help you to improve your cooking and make better use of your device.

Air Fryer

An air fryer is a kitchen tool that cooks food using much less oil than traditional cooking methods. Instead of using a large pot filled with oil, an air fryer uses heated air and a small amount of oil to cook your food. This helps keep your food healthy and minimizes the amount of fat you consume. The result is crispy, tasty food that is full of flavour. Most air fryers come in small compact sizes that are easy to store and can be used on the go. Most have an adjustable temperature setting that can be used to cook different types of food depending on what you're making. The time required for cooking is also significantly less compared to traditional methods so it can be a great time-saver. Additionally, most air fryers are easy to clean and maintain, making them a desirable kitchen tool for busy cooks.

How Do Air Fryers Work?

Ironically, an air fryer doesn't work by frying – the same way a deep fryer does – but more like a hot air convection oven fryer. The food in the air fryer is suspended, held in position by a perforated cooking basket, and hot air from the air fryer's fan circulates around the food. This produces a convection effect that cooks the food, making it brown and crisp.

The air fryer maintains the internal temperature at 160°C, which is enough to cook breaded foods such as frozen marinated chicken tenders and unbreaded foods such as French fries.

The air fryer cooks faster and can distribute heat more evenly compared to many other cooking appliances. You will also discover that preheating does not apply to all air fryers; some don't require it which makes them cook food even faster.

Unlike conventional ovens, air fryers are convenient in all seasons because they don't heat the house.

The Difference Between a Classic Fryer and An Air Fryer

A classic fryer uses oil as the cooking medium. Most people associate a deep-fry with a delicious snack or meal, but the use of excess oil and unhealthy trans fats makes deep frying unhealthy. The fat in the oil causes unhealthy amounts of fat to be consumed, which can increase the risk of heart disease and other health problems.

However, an air fryer uses hot air and circulation to cook food without the use of oil. It is a healthier alternative to the classic frying method, which uses unhealthy amounts of fat and trans fats to cook food. The absence of oil in the air fryer allows the food to be healthier and lower in calories. You will be able to enjoy the same great taste and texture of your traditional meals without all the unhealthy fats. The air in the air fryer is heated to around 160°C, which is enough to cook most foods. This is a healthier way to cook because the food is not submerged in fat, and the fat is not being transferred to your body.

Which Model to Choose?

There are many different air fryers on the market, so you need to shop around to find the best deal. Here are the main features of an air fryer you need to consider to help you narrow down your choices. You can also go online to read user reviews and learn more about the different models.

Loading: Each air fryer's model has a different size option. There are small models that will cook food for one to two people, medium models that will cook for two to four people, and large models that will cook for six or more people. The size of the air fryer you choose will depend on the number of people you will be cooking for.

Convenient: An air fryer should be simple and adaptable. Not everyone has the time to go through the user manual, although it is highly recommended that you do. Your air fryer of choice should also provide some ease of detaching and cleaning of the cooking basket.

Functionality: Depending on your needs, you can choose from many models that include things like built-in digital displays or those that allow you to monitor your cooking process through a simple window. Some models also come with pre-set cooking programs to choose from, such as a high or low setting.

Size: Air fryers should be big enough to cook food for 4 people. Most models can only cook for 2 at a time, therefore, requiring you to cook in batches for more people. That said, there are new models with an oven toaster that enable you to save your countertop space by replacing the toaster.

Electricity Consumption of An Air Fryer

While all models of air fryers use electricity to heat the air, the amount of power needed depends on several factors, including the amount of food being cooked, the type of food being cooked, and the power settings on your model. You will also want to consider the wattage of the air fryer to ensure you are not using too much power when cooking.

The usual cost to run an air fryer depends on the energy prices in your area and how long the air fryer is used each month. You can also find the estimated monthly cost of an air fryer on the manufacturer's website.

Cleaning And Maintenance of The Air Fryer

If you look after your air fryer well, it will last a long time. The key facts to remember are to clean you device often, but unfortunately, that means cleaning it after every use. This will help to get rid of any lingering food remnants that may otherwise clog up the machine and cause problems in the future. B sure to read the manufacturer's instructions to make sure that you cover all the bases and don' accidentally do something that could cause your air fryer to break.

A good point to remember is to avoid using anything abrasive when cleaning your air fryer. The insid walls can easily be scratched, and the coating is what helps to cook the food effectively. You can simpl use a soft cloth. Never submerge your air fryer unit in water - it's electric after all!

Whilst cleaning your air fryer after every use might be a boring job, you can work your way through i quickly with these instructions. Again, be sure to check your model's particular instructions just to mak sure that you are not accidentally doing anything wrong.

1.   After cooking, let your air fryer cool before thoroughly cleaning, and unplug from the mains.
2.   Clean the outside of your gadget with a damp cloth.
3.   Use a non-abrasive sponge and warm water to clean the inside, making sure that you get rid o anything that is stuck.
4.   Carefully tip the air fryer upside down to dislodge any pieces.
5.   Wipe the heating section carefully.
6.   If you can put your baskets and pans in the dishwasher (check instructions), you can do so, but i not, you can clean these with a soft cloth and water.
7.   Let everything dry completely before putting your appliance back together.

Tips For Using Your New Air Fryer

If you are a beginner with an air fryer, here are a few tips for using your new appliance to help you get th best results:

Preheat your air fryer for optimal results- Preheating your air fryer for 3 to 5 minutes is a goo practice to get the best out of your ingredients. It saves you time during the cooking process, and th taste and the look of your food will be better!

Avoid the smoke while cooking- Fatty food such as bacon, meatballs, lard, etc., can emit a lot of smoke while being cooked in an air fryer. You can add a bit of water under the air fryer basket to combat this. With this intelligent method, you kill two birds with one stone because you will also get the succulent taste of the meal and create the delicious gravy.

Grease the air fryer basket- Greasing your air fryer basket with a little oil is the secret to avoiding food sticking to the basket, which is a very annoying problem. This advice is highly recommended for lean foods that will release little fat during the cooking process.

Do not overload your air fryer- Your food is cooked by the air circulating in the basket, so it is essential not to overload your air fryer. Keeping room inside your air fryer basket will ensure you get a crispy and browned crust on most foods, so keep that in mind.

Shake helps to cook better- At the middle of the cooking cycle, shake the ingredients a little in the air fryer. As a result, your food will be perfectly cooked on each side.

Put enough space for large ingredients- It is better to space them out so that they do not overlap each other and you can still place a few small items in your air fryer at a time. This will help to keep heat distribution even and prevent food from burning on the outside while being raw on the inside. Also, make sure that you have more space around the air filter so that it can breathe freely.

Use a parchment paper when cooking messy ingredients- If you are cooking something messy like eggs, potatoes, etc., use parchment paper to avoid the mess from dripping in the air fryer. This will help to prevent the food from sticking to the basket and making it hard to remove from the machine. Just make sure that you remove the parchment when the food is completely cooked.

Sprinkle your food with oil before cooking it- Using oil spray on your food is the best way to make your food crispier and tastier.

Use bread slices to soak extra grease- If you don't have a foil to collect the extra grease at home, then you can solve the problem with bread; placing a slice of bread at the bottom of your air fryer is an easy way to catch extra grease and drips.

Never clean the air fryer in the dishwasher- An air fryer can be cleaned with regular water and detergent by disassembling the various components. Washing an air fryer in the dishwasher can damage it, so please be careful about that.

BREAKFAST

1. Breakfast Hash Browns

Preparation time: 15 minutes

Cooking time: 20 minutes

Servings: 2

Ingredients:

- 2 large potatoes, grated
- 1 tbsp bicarbonate of soda
- 1/4 tbsp salt
- 1/4 tbsp black pepper
- 1/4 tsp cayenne pepper
- 1 tbsp olive oil
- half of 1 chopped large onion
- half of 1 chopped red pepper
- half of 1 chopped green pepper

Directions:

1. Squeeze out any water contained within the potatoes and add it to a large water bowl.

2. Add the bicarbonate of soda, mix it well and leave to soak for 25 minutes. Drain the water away and carefully pat the potatoes to dry.

3. Transfer the potatoes to another bowl and add the spices and oil. Toss it well until combined.

4. Place the potatoes into your air fryer basket, set it to 200ºC, and cook for 10 minutes.

5. Shake the basket and add the peppers and onions. Cook for another 10 minutes and serve.

Nutrition: Calories: 246, Carbs: 42g; Fat: 3g Protein: 6g

2. French Toast

Preparation time: 5 minutes

Cooking time: 6 minutes

Servings: 2

Ingredients:

- 4 slices of sandwich bread
- 2 beaten eggs
- 2 tbsp softened butter
- 1 tsp each of cinnamon, nutmeg, ground cloves, & maple syrup
- Cooking spray

Directions:

1. Preheat your fryer to 180ºC.

2. Mix the eggs, salt, cinnamon, nutmeg, and cloves in a bowl.

3. Butter each side of bread and cut it into strips. Dip the bread slices into the egg mixture and arrange each slice into the air fryer basket.

.   Cook for 2 minutes, then take the basket
ut and spray with cooking spray.

.   Turn over the slices, and cook for 4
inutes. Remove and serve with maple syrup.
utrition: Calories: 159; Carbs: 51g; Fat: 35g;
rotein: 14g

3. Breakfast Lemon Blueberry Muffins

reparation time: 15 minutes

ooking time: 10 minutes

ervings: 12 muffins

ngredients:

315g self-rising flour

65g sugar

120ml double cream

2 tbsp of light cooking oil

2 eggs

125g blueberries

zest & juice of 1 lemon

1 tsp vanilla

Directions:

1.   Mix the self-rising flour and sugar in a small bowl.

2.   Whisk the oil, juice, eggs, double cream, and vanilla in another bowl. Mix this mixture with the flour mixture. Add the blueberries and fold in the mixture.

3.   Spoon the mixture into the silicone muffin mould and cook in your air fryer at 150ºC for 10 minutes. Remove, let it cool and serve!
Nutrition: Calories: 313; Carbs: 54g; Fat: 7.3g; Protein: 6.2g

4. Pancakes with Applesauce

Preparation time: 15 minutes

Cooking time: 6 minutes

Servings: 2

Ingredients:

- Cooking spray
- 2 eggs
- 60g flour
- 125ml milk
- Pinch of salt
- 1 tbsp of unsweetened apple sauce

Directions:

1.   Warm your fryer to 200ºC and place three ramekins into it.

2.   Blend all your ingredients inside a blender until smooth.

3. Grease your ramekins with cooking spray and pour the pancake mixture in each. Cook for 6 minutes, remove, and serve!

Nutrition: Calories: 139; Carbs:18g; Fat: 4g; Protein: 8g

5. Cheesy Bacon Toast

Preparation time: 10 minutes

Cooking time: 7 minutes

Servings: 1

Ingredients:

- 2 sandwich bread slices
- 1 cheddar cheese slice
- 1 mozzarella cheese slice
- 1 pre-cooked bacon slice
- ½ tbsp butter, melted

Directions:

1. Butter one side of each bread slice, and place one bread slice into the fryer basket.

2. Add the cheddar cheese, bacon, mozzarella cheese, and the remaining bread slice on top.

3. Cook it for 4 minutes at 170ºC. Flip and cook within 3 minutes. Enjoy!

Nutrition: Calories: 486; Carbs: 25g; Fat: 26g; Protein: 25g

6. Air-Fried Bagels

Preparation time: 5 minutes

Cooking time: 10 minutes

Servings: 1

Ingredients:

- 85g self-rising flour
- 60ml plain yoghurt
- 1 egg, beaten

Directions:

1. Mix the yoghurt and flour in your large bowl to create a dough.

2. Cover a flat surface with a little extra flour, place the dough, and create 4 even balls. Roll each dough into a log shape to form a bagel and brush the egg on top.

3. Arrange the bagels inside your fryer in one layer and cook at 170ºC for 10 minutes. Let it cool and serve!

Nutrition: Calories: 243; Carbs: 29.4g; Fat: 3g; Protein: 3g

7. Air-Fried Omelette

Preparation time: 5 minutes

Cooking time: 10 minutes

Servings: 3

Ingredients:

4 eggs

100ml milk

120g grated cheese

Salt, as needed

Directions:

1. Mix the eggs plus milk in your bowl, then flavour it with salt. Pour it into your greased pan inside your air fryer basket.

2. Cook at 170ºC for 10 minutes and sprinkle the cheese on top at the halfway point. Once done, serve and enjoy!

Nutrition: Calories: 220; Carbs: 15g; Fat: 3.5g; Protein: 12.9g

8. Cheesy Sausage Breakfast Pockets

Preparation time: 5 minutes

Cooking time: 10 minutes

Servings: 2

Ingredients:

• 1 packet of regular puff pastry, cut into rectangular shapes

• 4 sausages, cooked & crumbled into pieces

• 5 eggs, cooked & scrambled

• 50g cooked bacon

• 50g grated cheddar cheese

• 1 tbsp olive oil

Directions:

1. Scramble the eggs in a pan with oil over medium heat. Mix in the sausage and bacon. Move it to your plate.

2. Add a little of the egg and meat mixture to one-half of each pastry piece. Fold the rectangles and seal its sides.

3. Place your pockets into your basket and cook for 10 minutes at 190ºC. Let it cool and serve!

Nutrition: Calories: 234; Carbs: 33g; Fat: 4g; Protein: 2.4g

9. Breakfast Burritos

Preparation time: 15 minutes

Cooking time: 5 minutes

Servings: 6

Ingredients:

- 6 scrambled eggs
- 6 medium tortillas
- Half red pepper, minced
- 8 sausages, cut into cubes & browned
- 4 bacon slices, pre-cooked & cut into pieces
- 65g grated cheese
- A small amount of olive oil

Directions:

1. Combine the eggs, bell pepper, bacon, cheese, and browned sausage in a bowl.

2. Place enough of the mixture into the middle of your tortilla, folding up the top to bottom and rolling closed. Repeat until all your tortillas have been used.

3. Put the burritos into your basket and spray with oil. Cook the burritos at 170ºC for 5 minutes and serve!

Nutrition: Calories: 191; Carbs: 31.4g; Fat: 6g; Protein: 3.7g

10. Chorizo Potato Frittata

Preparation time: 5 minutes

Cooking time: 13 minutes

Servings: 1

Ingredients:

- 2 eggs
- Half of 1 chorizo sausage, sliced
- Half of 1 boiled potato, cubed
- 20g frozen sweetcorn
- Olive oil, as needed
- Feta cheese, as needed
- Salt & pepper to taste

Directions:

1. Grease your air fryer basket with olive oil then add the cubed potato, sweetcorn, and sliced chorizo. Cook at 180ºC for 8 minutes until the sausage is browned.

2. Beat the eggs and seasoning in your bowl and add it into your basket. Crumble the feta on top and cook within 5 minutes. Serve!

Nutrition: Calories: 421; Carbs: 17g; Fat: 26g; Protein: 27g

1. Eggs & Spinach Ramekins

Preparation time: 5 minutes

Cooking time: 20 minutes

Servings: 4

Ingredients:

- 500g wilted fresh spinach
- 4 eggs
- 1 tbsp olive oil
- 1 tbsp butter for cooking
- 4 tsp milk
- Salt & pepper to taste

Directions:

1. Preheat your air fryer to 180ºC.

2. Coat 4 small ramekin dishes with butter and arrange the wilted spinach, 1 teaspoon of milk, and 1 egg into each ramekin. Season with salt and pepper.

3. Cook in the air fryer for 20 minutes until the egg is cooked. Serve and enjoy!

Nutrition: Calories: 162; Carbs: 25g; Fat: 1g; Protein: 10g

12. Breakfast Stuffed Peppers

Preparation time: 5 minutes

Cooking time: 13 minutes

Servings: 2

Ingredients:

- 1 large bell pepper, deseeded & cut into halves
- 4 large eggs
- 1 tsp olive oil
- Salt & pepper to taste

Directions:

1. Rub olive oil on the edges of your peppers and crack one egg into each pepper—season with salt and pepper to taste.

2. Insert a trivet into your air fryer to hold the peppers and arrange the peppers evenly. Set your fryer to 200ºC and cook the stuffed peppers for 13 minutes. Serve!

Nutrition: Calories: 164; Carbs: 4g; Fat: 10g; Protein: 11g

POULTRY RECIPES

3. Sweet Citrusy Chicken

reparation time: 10 minutes

ooking time: 14 minutes

ervings: 2

ngredients:

600g chicken thighs, boneless and kinless

2 tbsp cornflour

60ml orange juice

2 tbsp brown sugar

1 tbsp soy sauce

1 tbsp rice wine vinegar

¼ tsp ground ginger

Pinch of red pepper flakes

Zest of 1 orange

2 tsp water & 2 tsp cornflour, mixed

irections:

1. Preheat your air fryer to 250ºC.

2. Combine the chicken and corn flour in a bowl. Add the chicken in your basket, and cook within 9 minutes. Set aside.

3. Mix the remaining fixings except for the cornflour mixture in your bowl. Pour it in your skillet, boil, and adjust to a simmer within 5 minutes.

4. Pour the cornflour mixture to your skillet, then mix it well. Pour this sweet citrus sauce on top of your chicken and enjoy!

Nutrition: Calories: 546; Carbs: 34g; Fat: 6g; Protein: 2g

14. Tandoori Chicken

Preparation time: 15 minutes

Cooking time: 15 minutes

Servings: 2

Ingredients:

- 500g chicken tenders, halved
- 1 tbsp each of minced ginger& garlic
- 1 tsp cayenne pepper
- 1 tsp turmeric
- 1 tsp garam masala
- 60ml yoghurt
- 25g coriander leaves
- Salt & pepper, as needed

Directions:

1. Combine all the ingredients except the chicken in a large bowl. Once combined, add the chicken and toss it well until fully coated.

2. Warm up the air fryer to 160ºC, put the tandoori chicken in your basket and baste it with oil. Cook within 10 minutes, turn it over and cook again within 5 minutes. Serve!

Nutrition: Calories: 178; Carbs: 2g; Fat: 6g; Protein: 25g

15. Chicken Meatballs

Preparation time: 20 minutes

Cooking time: 9 minutes

Servings: 4

Ingredients:

- 500g minced chicken
- 1 egg
- 1 tbsp dried oregano
- 1 ½ tbsp garlic paste
- 1 tsp lemon zest
- 1 tsp dried onion powder
- Salt & pepper, as needed

Directions:

1. Mix all the fixings in your large bowl and make the meatballs out of this mixture.

2. Preheat your air fryer to 260ºC. Add the meatballs in one layer to the air fryer basket and cook for 9 minutes. Serve and enjoy!

Nutrition: Calories: 346; Carbs: 34g; Fat: 6g; Protein: 19g

16. Chicken Buffalo Wings

Preparation time: 10 minutes

Cooking time: 30 minutes

Servings: 2

Ingredients:

- 200g chicken wings
- 35g butter
- 3 tbsp hot pepper sauce
- 1 tbsp vinegar
- ½ tbsp of olive oil
- ½ tsp of garlic powder
- cayenne pepper, as needed

Directions:

1. Warm your air fryer to 180ºC.

2. Add the chicken wings to your large bowl, drizzle it with oil, and toss until well coated. Put the chicken wings in your basket, and cook within 25 minutes.

3. Remove the basket, flip, and cook within more minutes. Transfer to your serving plate.

Stir the remaining fixings in your pan over medium heat. Serve the wings with the sauce on top. Enjoy!

Nutrition: Calories: 236; Carbs: 6.3g; Fat: 41.5g; Protein: 20.7g

7. Turkey Mushroom Burgers

Preparation time: 15 minutes

Cooking time: 10 minutes

Servings: 2

Ingredients:

180g mushrooms

500g minced turkey

1 tbsp of your favourite chicken seasoning

1 tsp each of onion powder & garlic powder

Salt & pepper to taste

Cooking spray

5 burger buns

Directions:

1. Process the mushrooms in your food processor, add all the seasonings, and mix it well.

2. Transfer mushroom to a bowl and add the minced turkey. Mix it well and shape it into 5 burger patties.

3. Grease it with cooking spray and put it in your basket. Cook at 160ºC for 10 minutes, flipping it halfway through until browned. Stuffed it between the burger buns and serve!

Nutrition: Calories: 132; Carbs: 25g; Fat: 26g; Protein: 25g

18. Buttermilk Marinated Chicken

Preparation time: 5 minutes

Cooking time: 10 minutes

Servings: 2

Ingredients:

- 250g chicken thighs, skinless & boneless
- 90ml buttermilk
- 20g tapioca flour
- ¼ tsp garlic salt
- 1 egg
- 35g all-purpose flour
- ¼ tsp brown sugar
- ½ tsp garlic powder
- ¼ tsp paprika
- ¼ tsp onion powder
- ¼ tsp oregano
- Salt, as needed
- pepper, as needed

Directions:

1. Mix the buttermilk and hot sauce in your bowl.

2. Add the tapioca flour, garlic salt, and black pepper to a plastic bag and shake it well to combine.

3. Meanwhile, stir the egg in your other bowl.

4. Dip the chicken thighs into the buttermilk one at a time, then in the tapioca mixture, egg, and flour.

5. Warm your air fryer to 190ºC.

6. Cook the buttermilk chicken for 10 minutes and enjoy!

Nutrition: Calories: 198; Carbs: 7g; Fat: 8g; Protein: 22g

19. Pepper & Lemon Chicken Wings

Preparation time: 10 minutes

Cooking time: 26 minutes

Servings: 2

Ingredients:

- 1kg chicken wings
- ¼ tsp cayenne pepper
- 2 tsp lemon pepper seasoning +1 tsp for the sauce
- 3 tbsp butter, melted
- 1 tsp honey

Directions:

1. Warm up your air fryer to 260ºC.

2. Combine the lemon pepper seasoning and cayenne in a bowl. Mix in the chicken until coated.

3. Put the wings in your basket and cook within 20 minutes. Turn the temperature up to 300ºC and cook for another 6 minutes.

4. Meanwhile, combine the butter, honey and the rest of the seasoning in a small bowl. Pour the sauce on the wings, and serve.

Nutrition: Calories: 356; Carbs: 31g; Fat: 6g; Protein: 8g

20. Buffalo Chicken Wontons

Preparation time: 15 minutes

Cooking time: 3-5 minutes

Servings: 6

Ingredients:

- 200g shredded chicken
- 1 tbsp buffalo sauce
- 4 tbsp softened cream cheese
- 1 sliced spring onion
- 2 tbsp blue cheese crumbles
- 12 wonton wrappers

Directions:

1. Warm up your air fryer to 200ºC.

2. Combine the chicken and buffalo sauce in a bowl.

3. Mix the cream cheese in another bowl until smooth. Add the scallion, blue cheese, and seasoned chicken and mix it well.

Run a wet finger along each edge of your wonton wrappers, place 1 tbsp of the filling into the centre and fold the corners together.

. Transfer it to your air fryer basket in one layer and cook at 200ºC for 3 to 5 minutes until golden brown. Serve and enjoy!

Nutrition: Calories: 463; Carbs: 9.4g; Fat: 34g; Protein: 24g

21. Quick & Easy Chicken Tenders

Preparation time: 10 minutes

Cooking time: 12 minutes

Servings: 2

Ingredients:

4 regular chicken tenders

1 egg, beaten

1 tbsp olive oil

75g dried breadcrumbs

Directions:

1. Warm your air fryer to 175ºC.

2. Place the beaten egg in your bowl.

3. Combine the oil and breadcrumbs in another bowl.

4. Coat the chicken into the egg one at a time, then cover it in the breadcrumb mixture.

5. Cook the tenders within 12 minutes and enjoy!

Nutrition: Calories: 250; Carbs: 9.8g; Fat: 11.4g; Protein: 26.2g

22. Chicken Fried Rice

Preparation time: 10 minutes

Cooking time: 20 minutes

Servings: 4

Ingredients:

- 400g cooked white rice
- 400g cooked chicken, diced
- 200g frozen peas and carrots
- 6 tbsp soy sauce
- 1 tbsp vegetable oil
- 1 diced onion

Directions:

1. Combine the rice, oil, and soy sauce in your bowl. Add the frozen peas, carrots, onion, and chicken. Mix it well.

2. Put the mixture into your pan fitted in your air fryer and cook at 182°C for 20 minutes. Serve!

Nutrition: Calories: 224; Carbs: 7.4g; Fat: 43g; Protein: 21.4g

23. Turkey Cutlets with Mushroom Sauce

Preparation time: 10 minutes

Cooking time: 11 minutes

Servings: 2

Ingredients:

- 2 turkey cutlets
- 1 tbsp butter
- 1 can of cream of mushroom sauce
- 160ml milk
- Salt & pepper to taste

Directions:

1. Preheat the air fryer to 220ºC.

2. Brush the turkey cutlets with butter, salt, and pepper. Put the cutlets to your basket and cook for 11 minutes.

3. Add the mushroom soup and milk to pan and cook for 10 minutes over medium heat stirring often.

4. Transfer the cooked turkey cutlets to you plate and top it with the sauce. Serve and enjoy!

Nutrition: Calories: 426; Carbs: 18g; Fat: 21g Protein: 16g

24. Chicken Schnitzel

Preparation time: 15 minutes

Cooking time: 6 minutes

Servings: 2

Ingredients:

- 150g chicken thighs, boneless, flattened
- 80g seasoned breadcrumbs
- ½ tsp ground black pepper
- Salt, as needed
- 15g flour
- 1 beaten egg
- Cooking spray

Directions:

1. Mix the breadcrumbs, salt, and pepper i your bowl. Place the beaten egg in another bow and the flour into your third bowl.

2. Dredge your chicken into the flour bow then in the egg, then evenly coat it in th breadcrumbs.

3. Put the chicken into your basket an grease it with oil.

4. Warm your air fryer to 190ºC and coo the chicken schnitzel for 6 minutes. Enjoy!

Nutrition: Calories: 234; Carbs: 5.6g; Fat: 21.5g;

Protein: 21g

BEEF, PORK, AND LAMB RECIPES

25. Beef & Vegetable Frittata

Preparation time: 15 minutes

Cooking time: 23 minutes

Servings: 2

Ingredients:

- 250g minced beef
- 4 shredded hashed browns
- 8 eggs
- Half a diced onion
- 1 courgette, diced
- 250g grated cheese
- Salt & pepper to taste

Directions:

1. Break the minced beef and place it in the air fryer basket. Add the onion and combine well.

2. Cook within 3 minutes at 260ºC, stir the mixture, and cook again within 2 minutes. Remove and clean the air fryer basket.

3. Add the courgette to the basket and spray with cooking oil. Cook for 3 minutes, add to the meat mixture, and mix it well.

4. Combine the cheese, hash browns, and eggs in a bowl. Add the meat and courgette and flavour it with salt plus pepper.

5. Add the mixture to a 6" round baking tray fitted in your air fryer and cook for 15 minutes. Cut into slices before serving.

Nutrition: Calories: 254; Carbs: 21g; Fat: 34g Protein: 14g

26. Roasted Rosemary Beef

Preparation time: 10 minutes

Cooking time: 45 minutes

Servings: 2

Ingredients:

- 200g beef fillet
- 1 tbsp olive oil
- 1 tsp salt
- 1 tsp rosemary

Directions:

1. Warm your air fryer to 180ºC.

2. Mix all the fixings in your bowl and transfer it in your air fryer basket.

3. Cook for 45 minutes and enjoy!

Nutrition: Calories: 293; Carbs: 25g; Fat:19g Protein: 29g

27. Beef Bulgogi Burgers

Preparation time: 40 minutes

Cooking time: 10 minutes

Servings: 4

Ingredients:

- 500g minced beef
- 2 tbsp gochujang
- 1 tbsp soy
- 2 tsp minced garlic
- 2 tsp minced ginger
- 2 tsp sugar
- 1 tbsp olive oil
- 1 chopped onion
- 4 burger buns for serving

Directions:

1. Combine all the fixings except for the burger buns in your bowl. Let it rest for at least 30 minutes in the fridge.

2. Divide the meat mixture into four and form it into patties. Put the burgers in your basket and cook within 10 minutes at 180ºC. Stuff it in the burger buns and serve!

Nutrition: Calories: 392; Carbs: 7g; Fat: 29g; Protein: 24g

28. Tahini Beef Bites

Preparation time: 15 minutes

Cooking time: 10 minutes

Servings: 2

Ingredients:

- 500g sirloin steak, cut into cubes
- 2 tbsp Za'atar seasoning
- 1 tsp olive oil
- 25g Tahini
- 25g warm water
- 1 tbsp lemon juice
- 1 clove of garlic
- Salt to taste

Directions:

1. Preheat the air fryer to 250ºC.

2. Combine the oil with the steak, salt, and Za'atar seasoning in a bowl.

3. Move it to your basket and cook within 10 minutes.

4. Combine the warm water, garlic, lemon juice, salt, and tahini in a bowl until well blended. Serve the beef bites with the prepared sauce on top.

Nutrition: Calories: 536; Carbs: 12g; Fat: 21g; Protein: 25g

29. Mustard Pork Tenderloin

Preparation time: 40 minutes

Cooking time: 25 minutes

Servings: 2

Ingredients:

- 1 pork tenderloin
- 3 tbsp olive oil
- 3 tbsp soy sauce
- 2 minced garlic cloves
- 2 tbsp brown sugar
- 1 tbsp Dijon mustard
- Salt & pepper, as needed

Directions:

1. Combine all the fixings excluding for the pork in your bowl.

2. Pour the mixture into a Ziplock bag, add the pork, and knead it well. Marinate it in you fridge for 30 minutes.

3. Warm your air fryer to 260ºC and plac the pork in your air fryer basket.

4. Cook for 25 minutes and enjoy!

Nutrition: Calories: 437; Carbs: 21g; Fat: 37.2g Protein: 31g

30. Pork Schnitzel

Preparation time: 10 minutes

Cooking time: 20 minutes

Servings: 2

Ingredients:

- 3 pork steaks, cut into cubes
- Salt & pepper to taste
- 175g flour
- 2 eggs, beaten
- 175g breadcrumbs

Directions:

1. Flavour your pork with salt and pepper Dredge it in your flour, then egg, and in you breadcrumbs.

2. Cook it in your air fryer at 175ºC for 2 minutes and enjoy!

Nutrition: Calories: 426; Carbs: 21g; Fat: 22g Protein: 21g

31. Brussels Sprouts Pork Chops

Preparation time: 10 minutes

Cooking time: 10 minutes

Servings: 4

Ingredients:

600g pork chops

Salt & pepper to taste

500g Brussels sprouts quartered

2 tsp olive oil

2 tsp maple syrup

2 tsp Dijon mustard

Directions:

1. Flavour your pork chops with salt and pepper.

2. Mix the oil, maple syrup, and mustard in a bowl. Mix in the brussels sprouts well until coated.

3. Cook both the pork chops and brussels sprouts in the air fryer at 200ºC for 10 minutes and enjoy!

Nutrition: Calories: 337; Carbs: 21g; Fat: 11g; Protein: 40g

32. Pork Taquitos

Preparation time: 5 minutes

Cooking time: 7 minutes, 10 seconds

Servings: 5

Ingredients:

- 400g shredded pork
- 500g grated mozzarella
- 10 flour tortillas
- Juice of 1 lime
- Cooking spray

Directions:

1. Warm up your air fryer to 190ºC.

2. Sprinkle the lime juice on the pork and mix it well. Microwave the tortilla for about 10 seconds to soften.

3. Add a little pork and cheese to each tortilla, roll it up to close, and place it in the air fryer basket.

4. Cook for about 7 minutes until golden. Serve!

Nutrition: Calories: 256; Carbs: 23g; Fat: 4g; Protein: 31.2g

33. Moroccan Lamb Patties

Preparation time: 5 minutes

Cooking time: 18 minutes

Servings: 2

Ingredients:

- 300g minced lamb
- 1 tbsp Moroccan spice
- 1 tsp harissa paste
- 1 tsp garlic puree
- Salt & pepper, as needed

Directions:

1. Mix all the ingredients all in your bowl. Form this mixture into patties and transfer them to your air fryer basket.

2. Cook for 18 minutes at 180ºC and enjoy!

Nutrition: Calories: 478; Carbs: 3g; Fat: 38g; Protein: 28g

34. Herbed Lamb Chops

Preparation time: 1 hour & 10 minutes

Cooking time: 7 minutes

Servings: 4

Ingredients:

- 454g lamb chops
- 2 tbsp of each olive oil & lemon juice
- 1 tbsp rosemary
- 1 tbsp thyme
- 1 tbsp oregano
- 1 tbsp salt
- 1 tbsp coriander

Directions:

1. Add all the ingredients except the lamb to a resealable bag and shake to mix well. Mix in the lamb chops, knead the bag, and marinate in your fridge for 1 hour.

2. Warm your air fryer to 198°C.

3. Cook the lamb chops for 7 minutes. Flip the lamb chops after 3 minutes of cooking time. Enjoy!

Nutrition: Calories: 414; Carbs: 1g; Fat: 37g; Protein: 19g

35. Lemon Crusted Rack of Lamb

Preparation time: 10 minutes

Cooking time: 30 minutes

Servings: 4

Ingredients:

794g rack of lamb

Salt & black pepper to taste

53g breadcrumbs

1 tbsp garlic clove, grated

1 tbsp cumin seeds

1 tbsp ground cumin

1 tbsp oil

¼ lemon rinds, grated

1 egg, beaten

Directions:

Warm your air fryer to 100°C.

Flavour your lamb with salt plus pepper. Keep it aside.

Mix the breadcrumbs, garlic, cumin seeds, ground cumin, oil, and lemon rinds in a bowl.

Dip your lamb in the egg, then roll it with the prepared breadcrumbs.

Cook the lamb for 25 minutes. Adjust the air fryer temperature to 200°C and cook the lamb for an additional 5 minutes. Let it cool and serve.

Nutrition: Calories: 400; Carbs: 4g; Fat: 24g; Protein: 44g

36. Lamb Spiced Meatballs

Preparation time: 10 minutes

Cooking time: 12 minutes

Servings: 2

Ingredients:

- 225g minced lamb
- ½ tbsp ground cumin
- 1 tbsp granulated onion
- 1 tbsp fresh parsley
- ¼ tbsp ground cinnamon
- Salt & black pepper, as required
- Cooking spray

Directions:

1.   Mix all the ingredients in your bowl. Make 2 ½ cm balls from this mixture.

2.   Lightly mist the meatballs with cooking spray and place them in an air fryer basket.

3.   Cook it within 15 minutes at 176°C and enjoy!

Nutrition: Calories: 328; Carbs: 1g; Fat: 22g; Protein: 27g

FISH & SEAFOOD RECIPES

37. Teriyaki Tuna Steaks

Preparation time: 5 minutes

Cooking time: 4 minutes

Servings: 2

Ingredients:

- 2 tuna steaks, boneless and skinless
- 2 tsp honey
- 1 tsp grated ginger
- 4 tbsp soy sauce
- 1 tsp sesame oil
- ½ tsp rice vinegar

Directions:

1.   Combine the fixings in a bowl except the tuna.

2.   Add the tuna steaks and toss them well until coated. Marinate it in your fridge for 3 minutes.

3.   Warm your air fryer to 270ºC.

4.   Cook the tuna within 4 minutes an enjoy!

Nutrition: Calories: 246; Carbs: 15g; Fat: 13.5g Protein: 22g

38. Paprika Lemony Shrimp

Preparation time: 15 minutes

Cooking time: 6-8 minutes

Servings: 4

Ingredients:

- 600g uncooked shrimp
- 2 tbsp olive oil
- 2 tsp pepper
- ½ tsp paprika
- ½ tsp garlic powder
- 2 sliced lemons
- juice of 1 lemon

Directions:

1.   Warm your air fryer to 200ºC.

2.   Mix all the ingredients in your bowl unt the shrimp is coated.

3.   Cook it for 6-8 minutes and enjoy!

Nutrition: Calories: 215, Carbs: 12.6g; Fat: 8.6g Protein: 28.9g

39. Thai Salmon Patties

Preparation time: 15 minutes

Cooking time: 8 minutes

Servings: 7

Ingredients:

1 large can of salmon, drained and bones removed

30g panko breadcrumbs

¼ tsp salt

1 ½ tbsp Thai red curry paste

1 ½ tbsp brown sugar

Zest of 1 lime

2 eggs

Cooking spray

Directions:

1. Mix all the ingredients in your bowl and form it into patties.

2. Preheat your air fryer to 180ºC.

3. Spritz your salmon patties using the cooking spray and cook for 4 minutes on each side. Serve and enjoy!

Nutrition: Calories: 533; Carbs: 24.3g; Fat: 22.5g; Protein: 14.7g

40. Crab Stuffed Mushrooms

Preparation time: 15 minutes

Cooking time: 18 minutes

Servings: 2

Ingredients:

- 500g large mushrooms
- 300g lump crab
- 50g Parmesan cheese, grated
- 2 tsp salt
- Half a diced red onion
- 2 diced celery sticks
- 35g seasoned breadcrumbs
- 1 egg
- 1 tsp oregano
- 1 tsp hot sauce

Directions:

1. Preheat the air fryer to 260ºC.

2. Arrange the mushrooms onto your baking sheet and grease it with oil.

3. Combine the onions, celery, breadcrumbs, egg, crab, half the cheese, oregano, and hot sauce in a bowl. Fill each mushroom with this mixture and ensure it is heaped over the top.

4. Cover with the rest of the cheese, place in your basket, and cook within 18 minutes. Serve and enjoy!

Nutrition: Calories: 146; Carbs: 15g; Fat: 11.5g; Protein: 32g

41. Butter Garlic Salmon

Preparation time: 10 minutes

Cooking time: 10 minutes

Servings: 4

Ingredients:

- 4 salmon fillets, boneless
- 4 tbsp melted butter
- 2 tsp garlic, minced
- 2 tsp parsley, chopped
- Salt & pepper, as needed

Directions:

1. Preheat the air fryer to 270ºC.

2. Combine the melted butter, parsley, and garlic in a bowl. Keep it aside.

3. Flavour the salmon fillets with peppe plus salt. Brush the salmon with the garli mixture on both sides.

4. Place the salmon with the skin side facing down into the air fryer basket and cook for 10 minutes. Serve and enjoy!

Nutrition: Calories: 207; Carbs: 21g; Fat: 18g Protein: 21g

42. Almond Crusted Tilapia Fillets

Preparation time: 10 minutes

Cooking time: 10 minutes

Servings: 2

Ingredients:

- 2 tbsp melted butter
- 150g almond flour
- 3 tbsp mayonnaise
- 2 tilapia fillets
- 25g thinly sliced almonds
- Salt & pepper to taste
- Cooking spray

Directions:

1. Mix the almond flour, butter, pepper, and salt in a bowl.

2. Brush the fish with the mayonnaise and coat it in your almond flour butter mixture Sprinkle sliced almonds on one side of your fish.

. Oil your air fryer basket using the cooking spray and cook the tilapia at 160ºC for 10 minutes per side. Serve and enjoy!

Nutrition: Calories: 724; Carbs: 13g; Fat: 59g; Protein: 41g

43. Squid Calamari

Preparation time: 10 minutes

Cooking time: 12 minutes

Servings: 2

Ingredients:

500g squid rings
500g panko breadcrumbs
250g plain flour
2 tbsp pepper
2 tbsp salt
200ml buttermilk
1 egg

Directions:

1. Combine the buttermilk and egg in your medium bowl.

2. Combine the salt, pepper, flour, and panko breadcrumbs in another bowl.

3. Soak the calamari into your buttermilk and roll it in your breadcrumbs.

4. Cook the calamari in your air fryer for 12 minutes at 150ºC and enjoy!

Nutrition: Calories: 426; Carbs: 25g; Fat: 21g; Protein: 21g

44. Nacho Crusted Crispy Prawns

Preparation time: 5 minutes

Cooking time: 8 minutes

Servings: 6

Ingredients:

• 1 egg

• 18 large prawns, patted dry

• 1 bag of nacho cheese flavoured corn chips, crushed

Directions:

1. Place the chips into a bowl and beat the egg in a second bowl. Coat the prawns into your egg and cover it with chips—Preheat the air fryer to 180ºC.

2. Place the prawns in your air fryer basket in one layer and cook for 8 minutes, shaking the basket halfway through cooking. Serve and enjoy!

Nutrition: Calories: 325; Carbs: 6.3g; Fat: 43.5g; Protein: 22.7g

45. Fish and Chips

Preparation time: 15 minutes

Cooking time: 30-35 minutes

Servings: 4

Ingredients:

- 2 fish fillets of your choice, cut into 4 slices
- 4 medium potatoes, peeled & sliced into chips
- 1 beaten egg
- 3 slices of wholemeal bread, grated into breadcrumbs
- 25g tortilla crisps
- 1 tbsp parsley
- 1 lemon rind and juice
- Salt & pepper, as required

Directions:

1. Warm your air fryer to 200ºC.
2. Cook the potato chips in your air fryer for 15-20 minutes. Set aside.
3. Meanwhile, drizzle the fillet with the lemon juice.
4. Process the breadcrumbs, tortillas, parsley, lemon rind, salt, and pepper into your food processor until crumbly.
5. Transfer to your plate, add the fillet and coat it evenly.
6. Cook the fillet at 180ºC for 15 minutes and enjoy!

Nutrition: Calories: 332; Carbs: 4.3g; Fat: 21.5g; Protein: 44.7g

46. Sweet Shrimp with Stir-Fry Vegetables

Preparation time: 10 minutes

Cooking time: 10 minutes

Servings: 2

Ingredients:

- 500g fresh shrimp
- 5 tbsp honey
- 2 tbsp gluten-free soy sauce
- 2 tbsp tomato ketchup
- 250g frozen stir fry vegetables
- 1 crushed garlic clove
- 1 tsp fresh ginger
- 2 tbsp cornflour

Directions:

. Pour the soy sauce, honey, tomato ketchup, garlic, and ginger in your pan. Simmer, add the cornflour and whisk until the sauce thickens.

. Coat the shrimp with the sauce. Prepare your air fryer basket using foil, then put in the shrimp and vegetables.

. Cook for up to 10 minutes for at 180ºC and enjoy!

Nutrition: Calories: 486; Carbs: 25g; Fat: 26g; Protein: 25g

47. Honey Sriracha Salmon

Preparation time: 10 minutes + marinating time

Cooking time: 12 minutes

Servings: 2

Ingredients:

25g sriracha

25g honey

• 500g salmon fillets

• 1 tbsp soy sauce

Directions:

1. Mix the honey, soy sauce, and sriracha in a bowl—Reserve half of the mixture for dipping.

2. Add the salmon and marinate for up to 30 minutes.

3. Oil your air fryer basket using cooking spray and warm your air fryer to 200ºC.

4. Cook the salmon fillets for 12 minutes and enjoy with the reserved sauce!

Nutrition: Calories: 246; Carbs: 5g; Fat: 13g; Protein: 21g

48. Butter Herbed Mussels

Preparation time: 10 minutes

Cooking time: 3-5 minutes

Servings: 2

Ingredients:

• 400g mussels, cleaned, soak in water for 30 minutes, & remove the beard

• 1 tbsp butter

• 200ml water

• 1 tsp basil

• 2 tsp minced garlic

• 1 tsp chives

• 1 tsp parsley

Directions:

1. Preheat the air fryer to 200ºC.

2.   Add all the ingredients to an air fryer-safe pan and cook for 3 minutes.

3.   Check to see if the mussels have opened; if not, cook for a further 2 minutes. Serve!

Nutrition: Calories: 100; Carbs: 4g; Fat: 3g; Protein: 11g

SIDES RECIPES

49. Air-Fried Okra

Preparation time: 2 minutes

Cooking time: 10 minutes

Servings: 2

Ingredients:

600g Okra, ends trimmed, & pods sliced

2 tsp olive oil

Salt & pepper, as needed

Directions:

. Warm your air fryer to 175ºC.

. Mix all the ingredients in your bowl and cook within 5 minutes. Toss and cook for 5 minutes. Enjoy!

Nutrition: Calories: 113; Carbs: 16.1g; Fat: 5g; Protein: 4.6g

50. Potatoes & Roasted Asparagus

Preparation time: 15 minutes

Cooking time: 5 minutes

Servings: 4

Ingredients:

• 4 young potatoes cut into small pieces, simmered & drained

• 454g asparagus, cut into small pieces

• 2 stalks scallions, chopped

• 4 tbsp olive oil

• 1 tbsp dried dill

• 1 tbsp salt

• ½ tbsp black pepper

Directions:

1. Toss the asparagus, scallions, and 2 tbsp of olive oil in a bowl. Put the asparagus to your basket and cook within 5 minutes at 176°C.

2. Mix the potatoes, roasted asparagus, scallions, remaining oil, dill, salt, and pepper in a bowl until well combined. Serve and enjoy!

Nutrition: Calories: 449; Carbs: 73g; Fat: 14g; Protein: 12g

51. Spicy Green Beans

Preparation time: 5 minutes

Cooking time: 12 minutes

Servings: 4

Ingredients:

- 300g green beans
- 1 tbsp sesame oil
- 1 tsp each of soy & rice wine vinegar
- 1 clove of garlic, minced
- 1 tsp red pepper flakes

Directions:

1. Warm your air fryer to 200ºC.
2. Toss all the ingredients in your bowl, cook the green beans for 12 minutes, and enjoy!

Nutrition: Calories: 59; Carbs: 6.6g; Fat 3.3g; Protein: 1.7g

52. Balsamic Bacon Brussels Sprouts

Preparation time: 2 minutes

Cooking time: 10 minutes

Servings: 4

Ingredients:

- 800g Brussels sprouts halved
- 2 tbsp avocado oil
- 4 tsp crumbled bacon
- 2 tsp balsamic vinegar
- 1 tsp pepper
- 1 tsp salt

Directions:

1. Warm your air fryer to 175ºC.
2. Mix all the fixings in your bowl except for the balsamic vinegar and bacon and cook for 5 minutes. Toss and cook for 5 minutes, then sprinkle with balsamic vinegar and bacon before serving.

Nutrition: Calories: 94; Carbs: 13.3g; Fat: 9.4g; Protein: 5.8g

53. Easy Potato Hay Sides

Preparation time: 25 minutes

Cooking time: 17 minutes

Servings: 4

Ingredients:

1 tbsp oil

2 potatoes, spiralized, soaked into water for 20 minutes, drained & patted dry

Salt & pepper, as nrequired

Directions:

1. Mix all the ingredients in your bowl.

2. Warm your air fryer to 180ºC.

3. Cook the potato hay for 5 minutes, toss and cook for another 12 until golden brown. Serve and enjoy!

Nutrition: Calories: 113; Carbs: 18.6g; Fat: 3.6g; Protein: 2.2g

54. Roasted Olive-Drizzle Garlic

Preparation time: 2 minutes

Cooking time: 20 minutes

Servings: 4

Ingredients:

4 head of peeled garlic

olive oil, as needed

Salt & pepper, as needed

Directions:

1. Drizzle the garlic with olive oil in your foil.

2. Cook it in your air fryer for 20 minutes at 200ºC. Flavour it with salt and pepper and enjoy!

Nutrition: Calories: 116, Carbs: 2g; Fat: 6g; Protein: 5g

55. Garlicky Herbed Potatoes

Preparation time: 2 minutes

Cooking time: 25 minutes

Servings: 2

Ingredients:

- 250g baby potatoes, quartered

- ½ tbsp oil

- ½ tsp salt

- ¼ tsp garlic powder

- ¼ tsp dried parsley

Directions:

1. Preheat the air fryer to 175ºC.

2. Mix all the ingredients in your bowl, cook it in your air fryer for 25 minutes, and enjoy!

Nutrition: Calories: 90; Carbs: 20.1g; Fat: 0.1g; Protein: 2.4g

56. Buttermilk Breaded Mushrooms

Preparation time: 15 minutes

Cooking time: 15 minutes

Servings: 2

Ingredients:

- Cooking spray
- 250g oyster mushroom
- 240ml buttermilk
- 188g all-purpose flour
- 1 tbsp olive oil
- 1 tbsp each of salt, black pepper, garlic powder, onion powder, smoked paprika, & cumin

Directions:

1. Preheat the air fryer to 190°C and spray the air fryer-safe pan with cooking spray.

2. Toss the mushroom and buttermilk in a bowl. Set aside within 15 minutes.

3. Mix the flour, and seasonings in your second bowl until well combined.

4. Coat the mushroom with the flour mixture, dip in the buttermilk, and coat with the flour mixture.

5. Arrange the mushroom on the pan in a single layer, leaving space between each mushroom—Cook in your air fryer for 5 minutes.

6. Brush the mushrooms with oil, then cook for 10 minutes. Serve and enjoy!

Nutrition: Calories: 356; Carbs: 58g; Fat: 10g; Protein: 12g

57. Garlic-Olive Brussels Sprouts

Preparation time: 2minutes

Cooking time: 8 minutes

Servings: 2

Ingredients:

- 225g brussels sprouts, trimmed
- 1 tbsp olive oil
- Salt & garlic powder, as needed

Directions:

1. Mix all the ingredients into your bowl.

2. Transfer the brussels sprouts to an air fryer basket and cook them at 187°C for about 8 minutes. Enjoy!

Nutrition: Calories: 110; Carbs: 11g; Fat: 7g; Protein: 4g

58. Quick & Easy Cherry Tomatoes Side

Preparation time: 2 minutes

Cooking time: 5 minutes

Servings: 2

Ingredients:

- 225g cherry tomatoes
- 1 tbsp olive oil
- ½ tbsp salt
- ¼ tbsp black pepper

Directions:

1. Mix all the ingredients into your bowl.

2. Cook the cherry tomatoes in your air fryer for 5 minutes at 149°C. Enjoy!

Nutrition: Calories: 133; Carbs: 19g; Fat: 7g; Protein: 1g

VEGAN RECIPES

59. Sweet Potato Cajun Balls

Preparation time: 5 minutes

Cooking time: 16 minutes

Servings: 2

Ingredients:

- 1 sweet potato, peeled, boiled & grated
- 1 tsp Cajun seasoning
- Cooking spray
- Sea salt, as needed

Directions:

1. Mix all the fixings in your bowl and form it into sweet potato balls.

2. Grease your air fryer basket using the cooking spray and cook the balls for 8 minutes at 200ºC. Toss the balls and cook for another 8 minutes. Enjoy!

Nutrition: Calories: 202; Carbs: 29g; Fat: 7g; Protein: 3g

60. Radish-Onion Paprika Hash Browns

Preparation time: 15 minutes

Cooking time: 13 minutes

Servings: 2

Ingredients:

- 150g radish, roots trimmed
- Half of 1 onion, peeled
- 1 tsp coconut oil
- ½ tsp onion powder
- ¼ tsp paprika
- Sea salt & ground black pepper, as needed

Directions:

1. Process the radish and onion in your food processor. Pour your coconut oil and stir them well.

2. Cook the hash browns in your air fryer for 8 minutes at 180ºC.

3. Put the onion and radish in a bowl, add the seasoning and mix it well. Cook the hash browns again for 5 minutes at 200ºC. Enjoy!

Nutrition: Calories: 116, Carbs: 5g; Fat: 6g; Protein: 15g

61. Courgette Chickpea Burgers

Preparation time: 15 minutes

Cooking time: 12 minutes

Servings: 2

Ingredients:

- Half of 1 courgette, grated & discard excess water
- 1 (250g) can of chickpeas, drained
- 1 spring onions, sliced
- 2 tbsp coriander
- ½ tsp of each chilli powder, mixed spice & cumin
- Pinch of dried garlic
- Salt & pepper, as needed

Directions:

1. Add the spring onion, chickpeas, courgette, and seasoning to the bowl. Make the burger patties from this chickpeas-courgette mixture.

2. Cook the chickpeas-courgette patties in your air fryer for 12 minutes at 200ºC and enjoy in a burger bun if you like!

Nutrition: Calories: 36; Carbs: 6g; Fat: 1g; Protein: 3g

62. Roasted Carrots Chunks

Preparation time: 2 minutes

Cooking time: 15 minutes

Servings: 2

Ingredients:

- 250g carrots, peeled & sliced into chunks
- ½ tsp olive oil
- ½ tsp cayenne pepper
- Salt & pepper, as needed

Directions:

1. Preheat your air fryer to 220ºC.

2. Add the carrots to a bowl with the olive oil and cayenne and toss to coat.

3. Cook the carrot chunks for 15 minutes, flavour it with salt and pepper. Enjoy!

Nutrition: Calories: 132, Carbs: 14g; Fat: 3g; Protein: 12g

63. Air-Fried Potato Wedges

Preparation time: 2 minutes

Cooking time: 20 minutes

Servings: 4

Ingredients:

- 4 potatoes, sliced into wedges
- 2 tbsp olive oil
- 4 tsp salt
- 4 tbsp rosemary, chopped

Directions:

1. Preheat the air fryer to 190ºC.
2. Drizzle the potatoes with oil and mix them with salt and rosemary in a bowl.
3. Cook the potato wedges for 20 minutes and enjoy!

Nutrition: Calories: 110; Carbs: 19g; Fat: 2g; Protein: 2g

64. Orange-Glazed Tofu

Preparation time: 40 minutes

Cooking time: 15 minutes

Servings: 4

Ingredients:

- 400g tofu, drained & cut into cubes
- 1 tbsp tamari
- 1 tbsp cornflour + 2 tsp, divided
- ¼ tsp pepper flakes
- 1 tsp of each minced ginger, fresh chopped garlic & orange zest
- 75ml of each orange juice & water
- 1 tbsp maple syrup

Directions:

1. Mix the tofu and tamari in your bowl. Mix in 1 tbsp cornflour and allow to marinate for 30 minutes.
2. Place the remaining ingredients into another bowl and mix it well. Set aside.
3. Cook the tofu for 10 minutes at 190ºC and add it to a pan with the prepared sauce mix and cook for 5 minutes until sauce thickens. Serve and enjoy!

Nutrition: Calories: 71; Carbs: 9g; Fat: 2g; Protein: 5g

65. Pesto Chickpea Pasta

Preparation time: 15 minutes

Cooking time: 12 minutes

Servings: 2

Ingredients:

- 100g vegan pasta, cooked & drained
- 50g basil leaves
- 6 artichoke hearts
- 2 tbsp pumpkin seeds
- 2 tbsp lemon juice
- 1 clove garlic
- ½ tsp white miso paste
- 1 can chickpeas
- 1 tsp olive oil

Directions:

1. Put the chickpeas in your basket, and cook within 12 minutes at 200ºC.

2. Blend the rest of the fixings in your blender until smooth except for the pasta.

3. Add the cooked pasta to a bowl and spoon over the pesto mix and chickpeas. Enjoy!

Nutrition: Calories: 400; Carbs: 41g; Fat: 23g; Protein: 18g

66. Tex-Mex Hash Browns

Preparation time: 15 minutes

Cooking time: 11 minutes

Servings: 4

Ingredients:

- 500g potatoes, cut into cubes, soaked in water for 20 minutes & drained
- 15ml olive oil
- 1 red pepper, sliced
- 1 onion, chopped
- 1 jalapeño pepper, sliced
- ½ tsp taco seasoning
- ½ tsp cumin
- Salt & pepper to taste

Directions:

1. Warm your air fryer to 160ºC.

2. Coat the drained potatoes using the olive oil. Put the potatoes in your basket, and cook within 18 minutes.

3. Mix the rest of the ingredients and potatoes in your bowl.

4. Cook the hash browns for 6 minutes in your air fryer, toss, and cook for 5 minutes. Serve and enjoy!

Nutrition: Calories: 186; Carbs: 33.7g; Fat: 4.3g; Protein: 4g

67. Lentil Carrot Burgers

Preparation time: 20 minutes

Cooking time: 1 hour & 15 minutes

Servings: 2

Ingredients:

- 50g black lentils
- Water, as needed
- 150g oats, pulsed into powder
- 50g white cabbage, chopped & steamed
- Half of 1 carrot, grated & steamed
- Half of 1 onion, diced
- ½ tbsp garlic puree
- ½ tsp cumin
- Salt & pepper, as needed

Directions:

1. Cook the lentils with water in your pan for 45 minutes until soft.

2. Mix all the ingredients in your bowl, mash, and make the patties.

3. Cook it in your air fryer for 30 minutes at 180ºC and enjoy!

Nutrition: Calories: 233; Carbs: 41g; Fat: 3g; Protein: 12g

68. Tofu Bowls

Preparation time: 20 minutes

Cooking time: 28 minutes

Servings: 2

Ingredients:

- Half of 1 block of tofu, cut into cubes
- 20ml vegan soy sauce
- 1 tbsp sesame oil
- ½ tsp garlic powder
- Half of 1 onion, chopped
- 1 tbsp Tahini dressing
- 1 bunch of baby Bok choy, chopped
- 150g quinoa
- Half of 1 cucumber, sliced
- Half of 1 carrot, shredded
- Half of 1 avocado, sliced

Directions:

1. Blend the sesame oil, soy sauce, garlic powder, and tofu in your bowl, then marinate it for 10 minutes.

Cook the tofu in your air fryer for 20 minutes at 200ºC.

2. Heat your pan with the remaining oil and cook the onions within 4 minutes. Add the Bok choy and cook within 4 minutes.

3. Place the quinoa in your bowl, add the vegetables, tofu, and Tahini dressing on top. Enjoy!

Nutrition: Calories: 552; Carbs: 25g; Fat: 26g; Protein: 25g

APPETIZERS

69. Cheesy Parsley Corn

Preparation time: 5 minutes

Cooking time: 14 minutes

Servings: 4

Ingredients:

- 4 corns on the cob
- 4 tbsp butter, melted
- 1 tsp dried parsley
- 4 tbsp parmesan cheese, grated
- Salt, as needed

Directions:

1.   Preheat the air fryer to 270ºC.

2.   Combine the melted butter, salt, and parsley in a bowl. Brush the corn with this mixture.

3.   Cook the corn for 14 minutes, remove and coat it with grated cheese. Enjoy!

Nutrition: Calories: 126; Carbs: 19g; Fat: 6g Protein: 3g

70. Aubergine Dip

Preparation time: 10 minutes

Cooking time: 12 minutes

Servings: 4

Ingredients:

- 1 aubergine
- 2 tsp oil
- 3 tbsp tahini
- 1 tbsp lemon juice
- 1 clove garlic minced
- salt & cumin to taste
- ¼ tsp smoked salt

Directions:

1.   Cut the aubergine in half lengthwise, coat in oil, and cook it in your air fryer for 12 minutes at 200ºC. Keep it aside.

2.   Spoon the aubergine flesh and blend with the remaining fixings in your food processor until slightly chunky. Serve.

Nutrition: Calories: 154; Carbs: 6g; Fat: 14g Protein: 3g

71. Camembert & Soldiers

Preparation time: 5 minutes

Cooking time: 15 minutes

Servings: 2

Ingredients:

1 piece of Camembert

2 slices of sandwich bread, toasted & cut into soldiers

1 tbsp mustard

Directions:

1. Preheat the air fryer to 180ºC.

2. Place the camembert in an air fryer-safe container and cook for 15 minutes.

3. Serve the camembert and soldiers with the mustard on the side.

Nutrition: Calories: 414; Carbs: 14g; Fat: 28g; Protein: 25g

72. Salty Potato Peels Snack

Preparation time: 2 minutes

Cooking time: 6-8 minutes

Servings: 2

Ingredients:

- Peels from 8 potatoes
- Salt, as needed
- Olive oil cooking spray

Directions:

1. Warm your air fryer to 200ºC.

2. Cook the potato peels greased with olive oil and flavoured with salt for 6-8 minutes. Enjoy!

Nutrition: Calories: 90; Carbs: 15g; Fat: 3g; Protein: 2g

73. Courgette Meatballs

Preparation time: 10 minutes

Cooking time: 10 minutes

Servings: 4

Ingredients:

- 400g oats, blend in your blender until crumbly
- 40g feta, crumbled
- 1 beaten egg
- Salt & pepper to taste
- 150g courgette
- 1 tsp lemon rind
- 6 basil leaves, thinly sliced
- 1 tsp dill
- 1 tsp oregano

Directions:

1. Preheat the air fryer to 200ºC.

2. Grate the courgette into a bowl and squeeze any excess water. Mix in the remaining fixings and create small balls from this courgette mixture.

3. Cook courgette meatballs for 10 minutes and enjoy!

Nutrition: Calories: 232; Carbs: 27g; Fat: 10g; Protein: 10g

74. Jackfruit Taquitos

Preparation time: 10 minutes

Cooking time: 33 minutes

Servings: 2

Ingredients:

- 1 large Jackfruit
- 250g red beans
- 100g Pico de Gallo sauce
- 50ml water
- 2 tbsp water
- 4 wheat tortillas
- Olive oil spray

Directions:

1. Cook the red beans, jackfruit, Pico de Gallo sauce, and water in your pan. Simmer within 25 minutes and mash it well.

2. Warm your air fryer to 185ºC.

3. Place the jackfruit red bean mixture to each tortilla and roll it to secure. Spritz it using the olive oil cooking spray, and transfer in your basket.

4. Cook Jackfruit Taquitos for 8 minutes and enjoy!

Nutrition: Calories: 326; Carbs: 25g; Fat: 26g; Protein: 25g

75. Cheesy Garlic Asparagus

Preparation time: 5 minutes

Cooking time: 7-10 minutes

Servings: 4

Ingredients:

- 1 tsp olive oil
- 500g asparagus, cut off the bottom about 1"
- 1 tsp garlic salt
- 1 tbsp grated parmesan cheese
- Salt & pepper to taste

Directions:

1. Preheat the air fryer to 270ºC.

2. Pat your asparagus dry and place it in the air fryer basket, covering it with the oil. Put the parmesan and garlic salt on top. Flavour it with salt plus pepper.

3. Cook for 7-10 minutes, flipping halfway through the cooking time. Add a little extra parmesan on top before serving.

Nutrition: Calories: 236; Carbs: 14g; Fat: 4g; Protein: 12g

76. Spicy Spanish Potatoes

Preparation time: 10 minutes

Cooking time: 23 minutes

Servings: 2

Ingredients:

- 4 large potatoes, sliced
- 1 tbsp olive oil

- 2 tsp paprika
- 2 tsp dried garlic
- 1 tsp barbacoa seasoning
- Salt & pepper to taste

Directions:

1. Mix all the ingredients in your bowl.

2. Cook the spicy Spanish potatoes in your air fryer for 20 minutes at 160ºC. Toss, adjust to 200ºC, and cook again for 3 minutes. Enjoy!

Nutrition: Calories: 234; Carbs: 40g; Fat: 7g; Protein: 5g

77. Orange Sesame Cauliflower

Preparation time: 40 minutes

Cooking time: 32 minutes

Servings: 4

Ingredients:

- 100ml water

- 30g cornflour
- 50g flour
- ½ tsp salt
- ½ tsp pepper
- 2 tbsp each of tomato ketchup & brown sugar
- 1 sliced onion

Directions:

1. Mix the flour, cornflour, water, salt, and pepper until smooth. Coat the cauliflower and chill for 30 minutes.

2. Cook the orange sesame cauliflower in your air fryer for 22 minutes at 170ºC.

3. Meanwhile, mix the rest of the ingredients in your pan, and cook for 10 minutes until thickened.

4. Mix the cauliflower with the sauce and top with toasted sesame seeds. Serve and enjoy!

Nutrition: Calories: 294; Carbs: 14g; Fat: 10g; Protein: 12g

78. Stuffed Jacket Potatoes

Preparation time: 15 minutes

Cooking time: 1 hour & 5 minutes

Servings: 4

Ingredients:

- 2 large russet potatoes
- 2 tsp olive oil
- 100ml yoghurt
- 100ml milk
- ¼ tsp pepper

- 50g chopped spinach
- 2 tbsp nutritional yeast
- Salt, as needed

Directions:

1. Warm your air fryer to 190ºC.

2. Massage the potatoes with olive oil, move it to your basket, and and cook within 30 minutes. Flip the potatoes and cook for 30 minutes.

3. Slice your potatoes into half, scoop the flesh and place in your bowl. Mash it with the yoghurt, milk, plus yeast. Add the spinach, salt and pepper, then mix well.

4. Transfer it into the hollowed potato and cook for 5 minutes at 160ºC and enjoy!

Nutrition: Calories: 250; Carbs: 43g; Fat: 5g Protein: 5g

79. Macaroni & Cheese Mini Quiche

Preparation time: 15 minutes

Cooking time: 20 minutes

Servings: 4

Ingredients:

8 tbsp macaroni pasta

1 block of shortcrust pastry

2 tbsp Greek yoghurt

2 eggs

150ml milk

1 tsp garlic puree

400g grated cheese

Directions:

. Flour the inside of 4 ramekins and put the pastry inside.

. Mix the yoghurt, garlic, and macaroni in a bowl and divide them into the ramekins.

. Mix the egg and milk in your small bowl, then pour over the macaroni. Sprinkle with cheese.

. Preheat the air fryer to 180ºC.

. Place the ramekins in your air fryer basket and cook them for 20 minutes until golden brown. Serve and enjoy!

Nutrition: Calories: 350; Carbs: 26g; Fat: 23g; Protein: 10g

SNACKS

80. Cheesy Carrot Garlic Chips

Preparation time: 5 minutes

Cooking time: 20 minutes

Servings: 4

Ingredients:

- 320g carrots, tops removed & cut into chips
- 2 cloves of garlic, crushed
- 30ml olive oil
- 4 tbsp grated parmesan
- Salt & pepper, as needed

Directions:

1. Mix the olive oil, garlic, and carrots chips in your bowl.
2. Add the parmesan and coat the carrots. Cook the cheesy carrot garlic chips in your air fryer for 20 minutes at 220ºC and enjoy!

Nutrition: Calories: 130; Carbs: 17g; Fat: 6g; Protein: 1g

81. Healthier Potato Fries

Preparation time: 10 minutes

Cooking time: 15 minutes

Servings: 4

Ingredients:

- 1kg potatoes, cut into sticks, soaked into water & dried
- 2 tsp olive oil
- ½ tsp salt
- ½ tsp pepper

Directions:

1. Grease the potato fries with oil in your bowl.
2. Put the potatoes in your basket, and cook within 15 minutes at 200ºC. Flavour it with salt and pepper and enjoy!

Nutrition: Calories: 147; Carbs: 29g; Fat: 3g; Protein: 4g

82. Asparagus Fries

Preparation time: 10 minutes

Cooking time: 6 minutes

Servings: 2

Ingredients:

12 asparagus spears

1 egg

1 tsp honey

100g breadcrumbs

Pinch of cayenne pepper

100g grated parmesan

75g mustard

75g Greek yoghurt

Directions:

1. Preheat the air fryer to 200ºC.

2. Combine the egg and honey in a bowl, then mix the breadcrumbs and parmesan on a plate.

3. Coat each asparagus in egg, then in the breadcrumbs. Cook the asparagus fries for 6 minutes.

4. Blend the rest of the ingredients in your bowl and enjoy it with the asparagus fries.

Nutrition: Calories: 312; Carbs: 44g; Fat: 8g; Protein: 19g

83. Onion Sweetened Dumplings

Preparation time: 15 minutes

Cooking time: 24 minutes

Servings: 4

Ingredients:

- 8 frozen dumplings

- 1 small onion, sliced

- ½ tbsp olive oil

- ½ tsp sugar

- Water, as needed

Directions:

1. Cook the dumplings in your skillet with enough water for 5 minutes, remove and drain well.

2. Oil the air fryer basket and preheat to 220ºC.

3. Add the onion to the air fryer-safe pan and cook for 12 minutes, stirring often. After 3 minutes, mix in the sugar, remove the onions, and place them on one side.

4. Cook the thawed dumplings to your air fryer for 4 minutes. Adjust to 270ºC and cook within 3 minutes.

5. Mix the dumplings with the onions before serving.

Nutrition: Calories: 109; Carbs: 8g; Fat: 6g; Protein: 4g

84. Garlicky Pumpkin Paprika Fries

Preparation time: 10 minutes

Cooking time: 15 minutes

Servings: 2

Ingredients:

- Half of 1 pumpkin, peeled, seeds discarded, & cut into sticks
- 5ml olive oil
- ¼ tsp paprika
- ½ tsp garlic powder
- Salt, as needed

Directions:

1. Combine all the fixings in your bowl.

2. Cook the garlicky pumpkin paprika fries for 15 minutes at 280ºC and enjoy!

Nutrition: Calories: 126; Carbs: 17g; Fat: 11g; Protein: 14g

85. Salty Garlic Almonds

Preparation time: 2 minutes

Cooking time: 6 minutes

Servings: 4

Ingredients:

- 2 tbsp soy sauce
- 2 tbsp garlic powder
- 2 tsp paprika
- ½ tsp pepper
- 800g raw almonds

Directions:

1. Mix all the ingredients in your bowl.

2. Cook the salty garlic almonds for 6 minutes at 160ºC, tossing every 2 minutes. Serve and enjoy!

Nutrition: Calories: 170; Carbs: 5g; Fat: 16g; Protein: 6g

86. Courgette Chips

Preparation time: 5 minutes

Cooking time: 12 minutes

Servings: 4

Ingredients:

250g panko breadcrumbs

100g grated parmesan

1 medium courgette, thinly sliced into chips

1 egg, beaten

Directions:

1. Warm your air fryer to 175ºC.

2. Mix the breadcrumbs and parmesan in your bowl. Dip the courgette chips into your egg, then into your breadcrumb parmesan bowl.

3. Spritz the courgette chips using the cooking spray, put it in your basket, and cook for 10 minutes. Toss, cook for 2 more minutes and enjoy!

Nutrition: Calories: 159; Carbs: 21.1g; Fat: 6.6g; Protein: 10.8g

87. Avocado Delicious Fries

Preparation time: 10 minutes

Cooking time: 7 minutes

Servings: 4

Ingredients:

- 2 ripe avocados, peeled & cut into fries
- 300g flour
- 200g panko breadcrumbs
- 2 eggs, beaten
- 2 tsp water
- 1 tsp black pepper
- ½ tsp salt

Directions:

1. Warm your air fryer to 200ºC

2. Combine the flour, salt, plus pepper in your bowl. Whisk the egg and water in your small bowl and put the breadcrumbs to your third bowl.

3. Coat the avocado fries in each bowl and spritz with cooking spray.

4. Cook for 4 minutes, flip the fries and cook within 3 minutes. Serve and enjoy!

Nutrition: Calorie: 319; Carbs: 39.8g; Fat: 18g; Protein: 9.3g

88. Hot & Spicy Potato Snack Wedges

Preparation time: 5 minutes

Cooking time: 18 minutes

Servings: 2

Ingredients:

- 1 potato, cut into wedges
- 1 tbsp olive oil
- ¼ tsp each of paprika, chilli powder, sea salt & parsley flakes
- ground black pepper, as required

Directions:

1. Warm your air fryer to 200ºC.

2. Combine all the ingredients in your bowl. Cook the potato snack wedges in your air fryer for 10 minutes.

3. Flip and cook for 8 more minutes until golden brown. Serve and enjoy!

Nutrition: Calories: 120; Carbs: 19g; Fat: 5.3g; Protein: 2.5g

89. Celery Root Fries

Preparation time: 10 minutes + soaking time

Cooking time: 10 minutes

Servings: 2

Ingredients:

- Half of the celeriac, cut into sticks
- 500ml water
- 1 tbsp lime juice
- 15ml olive oil
- 75g mayo
- 1 tbsp mustard
- 1 tbsp powdered horseradish

Directions:

1. Mix the water and lime juice in your bowl, soak the celeriac for 30 minutes, and drain well.

2. Warm your air fryer to 200ºC.

3. Mix the mayo, horseradish powder, and mustard in another bowl. Keep in your fridge for a while.

4. Drizzle the with oil and flavour it with salt and pepper.

5. Cook the celery root fries in your air fryer or minutes and serve with the prepared dip.

Nutrition: Calories: 168; Carbs: 13g; Fat: 12.9g; Protein: 1.8g

90. Butternut Squash Fries

Preparation time: 5 minutes

Cooking time: 22 minutes

Servings: 4

Ingredients:

- 400g butternut squash, cut into sticks
- 15ml olive oil
- 2 tbsp bagel seasoning
- 1 tsp fresh chopped rosemary

Directions:

1. Warm up your air fryer to 200ºC.

2. Drizzle the butternut squash with olive oil, then mix until well coated.

3. Add the butternut in your basket and cook within 22 minutes, stirring every 4 minutes. Sprinkle with bagel seasoning and serve!

Nutrition: Calories: 92; Carbs: 13.3g; Fat: 3.5g; Protein: 1.1g

DESSERTS

91. Pistachio Brownies

Preparation time: 10 minutes

Cooking time: 20 minutes

Servings: 4

Ingredients:

- 75ml milk
- ½ tsp vanilla extract
- 25g salt
- 25g pecans
- 75g flour
- 75g sugar
- 25g cocoa powder
- 1 tbsp ground flax seeds

Directions:

1. Combine all the dry fixings in your bowl. Mix the wet fixings in your second bowl. Mix both mixtures until well blended.

2. Preheat the air fryer to 175ºC. Line a 5-inch cake tin with parchment paper and pour the brownie mixture. Put it in your basket, and cook within 20 minutes. Serve!

Nutrition: Calories: 486; Carbs: 25g; Fat: 26g; Protein: 25g

92. Lemon Pies

Preparation time: 10 minutes

Cooking time: 10 minutes

Servings: 6

Ingredients:

- 1 pack of pastry, cut out into 6 circles
- 1 egg beaten
- 200g lemon curd
- 225g powdered sugar
- Half of lemon

Directions:

1. Preheat the air fryer to 180ºC

2. Add 1 tbsp of lemon curd to each pastry circle, brush the sides with egg, and fold.

3. Press around the sides using your fork to secure. Brush the pies with egg, put it in your basket, and cook within10 minutes.

4. Mix the lemon juice with the powdered sugar to make the icing and drizzle on the cooked pies. Serve and enjoy!

Nutrition: Calories: 646; Carbs: 45g; Fat: 26g; Protein: 25g

93. Apple Fritters

Preparation time: 15 minutes

Cooking time: 15 minutes

Servings: 4

Ingredients:

- 225g self-rising flour
- 200g Greek yoghurt
- 2 tsp sugar
- 1 tbsp cinnamon
- 1 apple peeled and chopped
- 225g icing sugar
- 2 tbsp milk
- Cooking spray

Directions:

1. Mix the flour, yoghurt, sugar, cinnamon, and apple in a bowl. Knead for about 3 -4 minutes, divide into four and flatten it.

2. Meanwhile, blend the icing sugar and milk in your small bowl and keep it aside.

3. Prepare your air fryer basket using parchment paper, then grease using the cooking spray.

4. Cook the apple fritters in your air fryer for 15 minutes at 185ºC. Drizzle with glaze and serve!

Nutrition: Calories: 305; Carbs: 66g; Fat: 1g Protein: 9g

94. Chocolate Shortbread Balls

Preparation time: 10 minutes

Cooking time: 14 minutes

Servings: 9 balls

Ingredients:

- 175g butter
- 75g caster sugar
- 250g plain flour
- 2 tsp vanilla essence
- 9 chocolate chunks
- 2 tbsp cocoa powder

Directions:

1. Warm your air fryer to 180ºC.

2. Combine the flour, sugar, cocoa butter and vanilla in your bowl, then knead the mixture into a smooth dough.

3. Divide the mixture into 9, place a chunk of chocolate in each piece, and form into balls covering the chocolate.

4. Cook the chocolate shortbread balls in your air fryer for 8 minutes at 180ºC. Toss the chocolate shortbread and cook for 6 minutes at 160ºC. Serve and enjoy!

Nutrition: Calories: 282; Carbs: 30g; Fat: 16g; Protein: 3g

95. Apple Blackberry Crumble

Preparation time: 5 minutes

Cooking time: 15 minutes

Servings: 4

Ingredients:

- 4 diced apples
- 150g frozen blackberries
- 50g brown rice flour
- 4 tbsp sugar
- 1 tsp cinnamon
- 4 tbsp butter

Directions:

1. Preheat the air fryer to 150ºC.

2. Mix the apple and blackberries in an air fryer-safe baking pan.

3. Mix the flour, sugar, cinnamon, and butter in a bowl, then spoon it over the apple and blackberry.

4. Cook the apple blackberry crumble in your air fryer for 15 minutes. Serve and enjoy!

Nutrition: Calories: 310; Carbs: 50g; Fat - 12g; Protein - 2g

96. Cherry Pies

Preparation time: 10 minutes

Cooking time: 10 minutes

Servings: 6

Ingredients:

- 300g prepared shortcrust pastry, cut into 6 pies
- 75g cherry pie filling
- Cooking spray
- 3 tbsp icing sugar
- ½ tsp milk

Directions:

1. Add 1 ½ tbsp cherry pie filling to each pie pastry, fold the dough in half and seal around the edges with a fork.

2. Put it in your greased basket, and cook within 10 minutes at 175ºC.

3. Mix the icing sugar and milk, then drizzle it over cooled pies. Serve and enjoy!

Nutrition: Calories: 686; Carbs: 28g; Fat: 27g; Protein: 21g

97. Lemon Tarts

Preparation time: 10 minutes

Cooking time: 15 minutes

Servings: 8

Ingredients:

- 100g butter
- 225g plain flour
- 30g caster sugar
- Zest and juice of 1 lemon
- 4 tsp lemon curd

Directions:

1.   Mix the butter, flour, and sugar in a bowl until it forms crumbs, then add the lemon zest and juice.

2.   Add a little water at a time until you have a dough. Roll out the dough and line 8 small ramekins with it.

3.   Add ¼ tsp of lemon curd to each ramekin and cook in the air fryer for 15 minutes at 180ºC. Serve and enjoy!

Nutrition: Calories: 318; Carbs: 27g; Fat: 10g; Protein: 3g

98. Chocolate-Dipped Balls

Preparation time: 15 minutes

Cooking time: 15 minutes

Servings: 6

Ingredients:

- 225g self-rising flour
- 100g sugar
- 100g butter
- 50g milk chocolate, melted
- 1 egg beaten
- 1 tsp vanilla essence

Directions:

1.   Mix the flour, butter, and sugar in a bowl. Mix in the egg plus vanilla to form a dough. Split the dough into 6 and form it into balls.

2.   Put it in your basket and cook within 15 minutes at 180ºC. Dip the cooked biscuits into the chocolate and serve!

Nutrition: Calories: 374; Carbs: 49g; Fat: 17g; Protein: 5g

99. Fruit Scones

Preparation time: 10 minutes

Cooking time: 8 minutes

Servings: 2

Ingredients:

- 225g self-rising flour
- 50g butter
- 50g sultanas
- 25g caster sugar
- 1 egg
- A little milk

Directions:

1. Combine the flour plus butter in your bowl. Add the sultanas and mix them well. Stir in the caster sugar.

2. Add the egg and mix it well. Add the milk until you have a dough. Shape the dough into scones.

3. Place in the air fryer and cook at 180ºC for 8 minutes. Serve and enjoy!

Nutrition: Calories: 374; Carbs: 57g; Fat: 12g; Protein: 8g

100. Wonton-Wrapped Banana Bites

Preparation time: 10 minutes

Cooking time: 6 minutes

Servings: 12 bites

Ingredients:

- 1 banana, sliced
- 12 wonton wrappers
- 75g peanut butter
- 1-2 tsp vegetable oil
- Water, as needed
- Juice from 1 lemon

Directions:

1. Mix the lemon juice, and water in a bowl. Add the bananas, and soak it for a while.

2. Place one piece of banana and a spoon of peanut butter in each wonton wrapper. Wet the sides and seal it.

3. Put the wrapped banana in your greased basket, and cook for 6 minutes at 190ºC. Serve!

Nutrition: Calories: 386; Carbs: 20g; Fat: 26g; Protein: 21g

Conclusion

The air fryer, a must-have fixture in any kitchen, is easy to use, fast to cook with, and ideal for adding a healthier touch to previously unhealthy foods. With the air fryer, you can make healthier, tastier food at a faster pace and with less grease than a traditional deep-fryer.

No matter your diet, air fryer cooking can be tasty and nutritious, and it's much healthier than using a traditional deep-fryer. This is an excellent guide to help you get started right and the best book on the market to help you understand how to use this revolutionary appliance to make healthier food and save time and money.

After completing this book and trying all the recipes we have provided, you will have a firm understanding of how to use your air fryer, and you will be well equipped to make the most of your air fryer, even if it is your first. You will have learned the ins and outs of air fryer cooking and how to make the most of your air fryer in ways you never thought possible.

We hope that you found this air fryer cookbook to be an interesting and informative read and that it has helped you discover the many ways you can use your air fryer to make healthier food without the extra grease.

Printed in Poland
by Amazon Fulfillment
Poland Sp. z o.o., Wrocław
13 December 2022

df761168-f430-409b-8313-5860e738452dR01